# Choosing a Caregiver:

## *Expect the Best*

## *and Know How to Ask for It*

by Haley Gray

Published by Best Seller Publishing®, Pasadena, CA
Edited by Samantha Herring

Best Seller Publishing® is a registered trademark

Printed in the United States of America.

ISBN-13: 978-1505615777
ISBN-10: 1505615771

This publication is designed to provide accurate and authoritative information with regard to the subject matter covered. It is sold with the understanding that the publisher is not engaged in rendering legal, accounting, or other professional advice. If legal advice or other expert assistance is required, the services of a competent professional should be sought. The opinions expressed by the authors in this book are not endorsed by Celebrity Press® and are the sole responsibility of the author rendering the opinion.

Most Best Seller Publishing® titles are available at special quantity discounts for bulk purchases for sales promotions, premiums, fundraising, and educational use. Special versions or book excerpts can also be created to fit specific needs.

For more information, please write:
Best Seller Publishing®
1346 Walnut Street, #205
Pasadena, CA 91106
or call 1(626) 765 9750
Toll Free: 1(844) 850-3500

Visit us online at: www.BestSellerPublishing.org

*Your guide to finding*
*trusted, compassionate,*
*and qualified care*
*for aging parents*

*This book and the home care agency I founded evolved from the road I traveled while caring for my aging parents. This book is framed by our story. You may find yourselves in a similar position. Or you may be trying to figure out how to best care for a child with a disability, or perhaps you are an adult with a disability who needs a little extra help. This book is for every person seeking care they can trust, whoever and wherever they are.*

—Haley Gray, Founder of The Extension of You Home Care

# Table of Contents

# An Introduction

When I began the journey that led to this book, I was a busy mother of four children and was working full-time outside the home. I was also responsible for taking care of my elderly parents, as they were no longer capable of taking care of themselves.

In 2005, my parents decided to move from Alabama to North Carolina so they could be closer to their grandchildren and the rest of the family. Once they were closer, we were able to see them more regularly, and it became clear very quickly that both of them had health issues, particularly Dad.

Mom had been living with multiple sclerosis for almost two decades before this move, and she had extensive healthcare needs. Dad was the one who was responsible for providing her care and seeing to her needs for most of those twenty years. Mom's health had been the constant focal point in their lives and as a result, we hadn't really noticed the changes in Dad's health.

After the move, his health started declining quickly and noticeably. His ability to follow a conversation, pay bills, do mathematical calculations, and remember things started to decline. When he walked, his movements were stiff and jerky, and he held his cane at a funny angle. We noticed that the house was no longer being kept as clean as it should have been.

It took many medical appointments, lots of back and forth with different doctors and neurologists, and a couple of hospitalizations before he was eventually diagnosed with Parkinson's disease. After the hospitalizations, we began to occasionally use home care services. Dad suffered frequent falls at home and would call us in the middle of the night asking us to come pick him up from the floor. As his health deteriorated further, we started using home care more and more.

We began talking with different agencies to find out what services were available. We ended up working with several agencies, and during the next five years we had a number of different caregivers coming in and out of his home.

As a result, I learned a great deal about the caregiving industry as a whole and how it worked. I started asking caregivers about their motivations: why they were in this field, how they felt about their employers, and how they felt about time-keeping, worker pay, patient charting, and other aspects of their jobs. I even asked why they did things a certain way, like how they changed adult diapers. Many of them were very forthright and open with their opinions about ways the home care industry could be improved.

I asked a lot of nosy questions about how caregivers were paid and how their taxes were handled. In other words, I spent a lot of time interviewing them. Through many conversations over the course of several years, I started to see quite a few opportunities for positive changes in the field.

It appeared that both the employees and the clients were often treated in an impersonal way instead of as valued persons. Agencies didn't seem to use much discernment in matching caregivers to clients. They were more or less randomly assigned based on availability. Unless the agency received a complaint, the assigned caregiver would remain in place as long as they were with the agency.

Unfortunately, in many cases seniors don't know that they have the right to complain if their caregiver does a less than stellar job. If the patient has dementia, the problem is compounded. Dad had dementia, so he wasn't able to complain if his caregiver was not doing her or his job properly. We would only find out that a caregiver had left him unattended for several hours because someone else in the facility would tell us about it; Dad was not able to remember that he had been left alone.

At the time I was taking care of my parents, I made the decision to enroll in Duke University's Fuqua School of Business and complete a master's degree in business administration. I was especially interested in the Entrepreneurship and Innovation concentration. For the required final project, I chose to create a business plan for my own home care business. Using basic business principles and analysis, I wanted to be able to prove that a company could build a successful caregiving agency by taking good care of clients *and* employees.

Caregivers are commonly expected to give their whole heart to the job while being paid as little as possible and being granted no sick time or paid time off. This can have a substantial negative effect on the quality of treatment clients receive.

We had a number of incidents with Dad's care that were frankly terrifying. We once had a caregiver leave him unattended for three hours while on the clock because she went to pick up a friend from the train station.

We also found that some caregivers were not bathing or changing him properly: sometimes he would be left sitting in a soggy incontinence brief for hours on end. Unfortunately, Dad was extremely prone to urinary tract infection (UTI), and any time he was left sitting in a soggy brief it increased the risk of infection. Every time he had a urinary tract infection, he would become delusional, run a fever, and become incoherent. As infections repeatedly occurred, he began to develop bacterial infections that were resistant to antibiotics, and we were increasingly less able to treat the urinary tract infections as they emerged. Every infection was worse than the previous one, and we saw a marked decline in his health.

Compounding the issue, urinary tract infections are harder on the elderly than on a younger person. They can permanently damage kidneys or cause a life threatening blood infection. UTI's can also cause the elderly to become confused and agitated, have poor motor skills, and even cause them to hallucinate. Clients who already have dementia—like my dad did—find the dementia is exponentially intensified when they get a urinary tract infection. Their cognitive ability can suffer so much that they can't feed or dress themselves. In Dad's case, he essentially became catatonic; he had to be fed, dressed, bathed, and taken care of because he couldn't understand anything going on around him, and he certainly couldn't help. Though conscious, he would babble incoherently.

It seemed that Dad would get a urinary tract infection every single time we got a new caregiver who was less than exemplary, which was unfortunately almost every single time a fill-in caregiver was sent out.

When we had caregivers who were conscientious about making sure that Dad's clothes were clean, the incontinence briefs were changed, and he was bathed and toileted properly, the recurrence of these infections dropped significantly and his cognitive skills would actually improve quite a bit. He would start walking better and get up and about. He would go play bridge and have a social life. In other words, his health very much depended on the level of care he received.

When Dad had the right caregiver, his clothes always looked very neat, his presentation was always very proper, and he smelled wonderful. In fact, his favorite caregivers had special lotions, body washes, soaps, and such that they enjoyed sharing with him. They liked for him and his home to smell nice. It was an ongoing source of amusement with the family because some the caregivers had so much fun keeping him well groomed and immaculately presented.

In all likelihood, his life was prolonged quite a bit because we were able to locate and retain a few very good caregivers who remained his primary caregivers for about two years. The quality of care that those caregivers provided made a tremendous difference in the quality of his life. During that time, he went from being almost completely unable to get out of his wheelchair and walk to being able to walk with a cane.

My experiences with both poor and excellent caregivers greatly influenced my desire to found Extension of You Home Care. I saw conditions such as low pay, no benefits, and lack of supervision, under which caregivers labored to provide care. When you pay an employee a less than adequate salary, they are likely to feel undervalued and lack the motivation to perform at their best.

Most talented caregivers consider their work a higher calling—a gift that they feel driven to share with others. They want to take care of others. Every improvement a caregiver agency can provide to its staff reaps exponential benefits. A reasonable wage, health benefits, paid time off, and compassionate employers can generate more satisfied employees. Better-satisfied employees means better overall care. This is the underlying foundation of the business plan I created. Pay employees appropriately competitive salaries, classify them as W-2 employees as opposed to contractors, and offer some level of benefits such as paid time off, a 401K, and educational opportunities. This approach can increase employee loyalty *and* client satisfaction. That means you'll have less employee turnover and more knowledgeable employees. A well cared-for, satisfied customer generally tends to stay in better health and remain a client longer. That translates to better outcomes in terms of quality of life and length of life for clients.

I have constantly felt called to help other people throughout my life. I have a strong commitment to community service and saw an opportunity to expand my ability to help others by writing this book. I want others to learn from some of the mistakes I made while choosing home care services and caregivers.

I do consider caregiving to be a higher calling. I felt moved in this direction years before I took the leap and started Extension of You Home Care.

This book is especially meant to help adult children who find themselves with the responsibility of having to find caregivers for their parents. This responsibility can sometimes come about quite suddenly, leaving a person at quite a loss about what to do. Perhaps your parent is about to be discharged from the hospital and is no longer able to live independently. Maybe you visited their home for a holiday and you suddenly realized that the house isn't as clean as it should be, the fridge is empty, and the cat's litter box is overflowing. In other words, you start to notice that things are not going the way they should anymore.

The cost of care in an assisted living facility can be financially challenging for some, or sometimes parents just don't want to move to a new environment. Sometimes a little bit of extra help around the house—or home care—can help them remain independent and at home a while longer.

This book will help you understand why it is important to choose the right agency or provider and how to do so. It will give you an overview of the different kinds of care that are available. You will learn why it is important to ask a lot of questions when you interview a provider and what questions you need to ask.

# Children and Parents—Changing Roles

Roles between parents and children change over time. As parents age, the average parent-child relationship gradually evolves as the child increasingly has to make decisions for the aging parents.

It can be extremely disconcerting to experience this shift in the relationship. We think, "This isn't the way things are supposed to be. Our parents are supposed to be *our* caregivers, authority figures, and decision makers."

Unfortunately, that's not how it always works out. Children caring for their parents almost always have to start taking a more parent-like role. They have to oversee everything from living arrangements and groceries to medication, doctors' appointments, and clothing purchases. Essentially, many end up having to make most of the decisions about their parents' lives. These can be daunting responsibilities when adult children are already trying to balance very full lives that may include children of their own, work, school, and other family members that need care.

As Dad's dementia progressed, I was forced to be the adult in our relationship. One of the difficulties with dementia is that it is a progressive disease that doesn't always seem to be as serious from one day to the next. For instance, one day Dad might be able to play bingo or bridge. The next, he might not be able to remember where to put the markers on the bingo card. Some days he could feed himself, and others he couldn't figure out how to use a fork. Sometimes skills would come back, and sometimes they wouldn't.

While persons with dementia continue to have periods of lucidity, they retain the legal right to make their own decisions. The state will not easily remove that right. Proving that someone is incompetent to make his or her own decisions is quite hard.

Caring for a parent can be a very difficult tightrope walk. You have to make decisions for somebody who may or may not agree to let you. Your loved one may be making poor decisions with detrimental long-term consequences because they can no longer understand the effects of their decisions. How often do we hear about seniors giving money away to strangers or being duped by con artists? Identity thieves, telemarketers, and scam artists prey on the aged. We want to protect them from that, even though they may not think they need our help.

### Establishing Rules

At a certain point, it becomes necessary to establish certain rules. After my mom passed away, it seemed every woman in the facility where my dad lived wanted to have meals with him, date him, or become intimate with him. They even had fights over him. They circled around him to see who could get to him first. Dad enjoyed all the attention; he enjoyed dating and living a single lifestyle. He loved the women, and they loved him.

Things got very awkward, however, when one of his relationships progressed to sexual intimacy. We felt obligated to bring up the subject of safe sex. His response was, "Well, she can't get pregnant." Surprisingly, the senior community has one of the highest rates of sexually transmitted diseases (STDs) of all demographics. According to the CDC[1], diseases like Syphilis and Chlamydia increased by 52 and 31 percent respectively from 2007 to 2011. This puts seniors in competition with

---

[1] nytimes.com "Sex and the Single Senior" by **Ezekiel J. Emanuel Pub. Jan 18, 2014**

young people between the ages of 20 and 24 in terms of the biggest increase in STDs.

Given those statistics, seniors should be concerned about sexually transmitted diseases. STDs are rampant in nursing homes because inhibitions simply aren't there—go figure.

Who ever thinks that they'll need to lecture a parent about safe sex? When did that become a necessity, right? Eventually, we started making rules to protect Dad's safety, the safety of his caregiver, and the safety of the rest of us.

We had to make a rule that he was not allowed to visit his girlfriend's apartment. He would insist on sitting on her couch, and once he did, he would get stuck there. He weighed about 240 pounds, and he couldn't get himself back up. Someone else— his caregiver, his girlfriend, or anybody available—ended up having to go in to pull and lift him off of the couch. Unfortunately, several times his girlfriend or caregivers injured themselves trying to help him up.

We ended up having to put several rules in place concerning his lifestyle: because of his health, no alcohol was allowed; he had an allotment of money he could spend each week; and we had some say about when and how he was allowed to go out with his girlfriend (for safety reasons). We had to make sure that he stayed safe and didn't give all of his money away. Dad's reaction to some of these rules made us feel like a parent dealing with a surly child. Other times, he seemed like a teenager who had just discovered the excitement of dating.

Whether you are providing hands-on care or helping from a distance, being placed in the position of caring for a parent can be bewildering. You are forced to make decisions that you never thought you'd have to make. Take solace in knowing that role reversals are a normal part of the aging process. They are challenging, but often necessary.

### Discuss Your Parents' Wishes Before It's Urgent

Don't ignore the elephant in the room. Understanding your parents' wishes while they are still of sound mind can make things much easier. Understand how they want to be cared for, under what circumstances they would want to be kept alive or not, and what things are and are not important to them. Dad felt very strongly about keeping his pets with him until the very end, so we made sure his cat remained with him until he passed away. We focused on his quality of life as long as we could, making every effort to keep him happy and healthy as long as possible. In the end, I had to make some tough decisions, but it was very helpful to know that we had already clarified his wishes and defined what they were when he was in a much more clear state of mind. Because of this, I was able to follow his wishes even when he could no longer communicate them.

Don't just get an understanding of whether your parents prefer home care over a nursing home, but get a grasp on the full picture of what they would really want. For instance, Dad said he never wanted to go to a so-called "nursing home." The care industry can change dramatically from one generation to the next, or even in the course of a few years. And things *did* change from the time my dad first told me he didn't want to live in a nursing home. Assisted living facilities began providing levels of care that could have only been provided in nursing homes before. In some ways, the whole definition of what a nursing home *is* has changed. The kind of care that used to be provided exclusively by nursing homes has branched out to other types of care providers such as assisted living and home-care providers.

As uncomfortable as it may be to discuss end-of-life decisions, not discussing them can have undesirable impacts, both emotionally and financially. If not discussed ahead of time, decisions might be made based purely on emotion and not on what the dying person would have actually wanted. For those having to make the decisions, this time is difficult enough without having to live with the worry of whether or not they did the right thing.

Of course, it's preferable to have these discussions when your parents are healthy and the matter is not urgent. Unfortunately, we don't often talk about these things until we are forced to face them. That can be a big problem. Sitting down together and talking these matters over when everyone is relaxed is a much better idea. You could even start these discussions as soon as you are out on your own and independent from your parents—even if you are only in your twenties—because sometimes things can happen unexpectedly.

If your parents have progressed to the point that they are not able to discuss these matters, sit down with your siblings or other family members, and try to understand what your parents would have liked. Then, based on your parents' financial resources, you can create a plan of care for your parents whether or not they can articulate exactly the type of care they want. If they have dementia or are unable to tell you their wants and needs, you have to make the decisions to the best of your ability. If you have conversations about their care early and often, you'll be in a much better position to make those decisions.

Keep in mind that people's desires, resources, and what they want may change over time. The options available can also change dramatically over time, which makes it important to have continuing discussions about your parents' wishes and to understand the motivations behind what they want as well. If you understand their thought processes and motivations, making changes to their care plan becomes less stressful.

Many times parents feel strongly about not wanting to be a burden to their children. If your parent expresses these feelings, talk through what that means to them and what it means to you. Help them understand that you want to take care of them, and that addressing the issue of care now does take some of the burden off of you. Explain that "not being a burden" can mean taking care of themselves proactively and seeking out the care that they need. My dad was adamant about wanting to leave me an inheritance, so he really hated having to pay for any kind of care. We had to have some difficult discussions. I needed him to take care of himself and Mom by hiring a caregiver, rather than relying on me to provide all of the assistance that they needed and wanted. In my case, it was a discussion that we had to have several times. I was not able to gain his cooperation until he was discharged from rehab and moved to an independent living facility. I came to realize that my parents would eventually dismiss any caregiver taking care of them while they were still at home but were willing to accept help if they were in a facility. Sometimes you have to get creative to find a solution that works for everyone.

### *Lean on Others*

I found it helpful to talk to other people who had been through or were going through what we were. It was comforting to know that we were not alone—and we were not. The number of persons over 65 years of age is expected to double from 2000 to 2030[1]. With the number of seniors increasing so quickly, there will be a lot of adult children out there dealing with the same issues. You don't have to start from scratch and create an entirely new method of taking care of your parents. Chances are you can look to those who have already been there for guidance. Look for a caregiver support group in your community.

It's worth repeating: for every obstacle that I hit, I felt incredibly alone. People don't talk about the challenges associated with caring for aging parents. The more I talked about it and the more questions I asked my network, the more resources I discovered. Friends helped me find a geriatric care manager, a geriatric pharmacist, and a good home care company. Start reaching out and asking for help. So many people are willing to help you; you just have to find them.

# Understanding Levels of Service

The level of service needed for any particular client should be determined during an assessment by a qualified professional. Typically, that professional will be a registered nurse or a social worker. It should be someone who has had many years of experience determining the appropriate level of care for clients.

The program of care is mapped out during an in-depth assessment. A professional will determine the client's needs and the family's desires: help around the home; laundry; food preparation; medication reminders or medication administered; medical or non-medical home care; physical therapy, speech therapy, or occupational therapy; or personal hygiene needs such as somebody to bathe them, brush their teeth, dress them, and toilet them. Every aspect of the client's life is looked at carefully. It is important to understand what the agency recommends for the client and to have a very clear and concise care plan.

Let's start by defining the two main umbrella terms usually associated with home care.

### Home Health Care

Home health care typically involves medical care. That care can be provided by a CNA (Certified Nursing Assistant), physical therapist, nurse, occupational therapist, speech therapist, or other medical care provider depending on the client's needs.

This type of care typically requires a doctor's orders and for many people is covered by health insurance, Medicare, or Medicaid.

Those receiving home health care for the first time often have the misconception that they are going to receive extensive care at home. However, what home health care typically means is that the client will receive several visits per week by a provider. The visits may be anywhere from thirty minutes to an hour or so to help with things like bathing, dressing and physical therapy. These are not long visits. The person providing care will not prepare meals, clean, or spend large blocks of time with the client.

Some clients who receive home health care may need additional companion home care as well. The services provided through home health care may not be sufficient to meet all of their everyday needs. A lot of people are caught off guard by how little time a health care provider actually spends with a client. I made that discovery when caring for my parents.

### Home Care

Home care is typically non-medical personal care. It can include CNA care, companion care, personal care, transportation services, and respite care. This kind of care is usually not covered by insurance and is typically a self-pay service (clients pay for these expenses out of their own pocket).

In some exceptional cases, there may be coverage through Medicare, Medicaid, or other insurances.

Now, let's take a look at some of the different *levels* of care.

### Companion Care

Companion care means that there is absolutely no hands-on care. Caregivers can come in and do things such as laundry, housekeeping, meal preparation, keeping company, giving medication reminders (which means to remind somebody to take their medication) and driving a client to a doctor's appointment. They help keep a client safe. Companions can even supervise a shower. While they can hand the soap to the client when the client is in the shower, they cannot help the clients wash themselves.

Coverage for this type of care can range from a one-hour shift up to 24 hours per day. The amount of time depends on the client's needs. Some need just a little bit of help while others need more. For example, clients with dementia need somebody to keep them safe from wandering during the night, so families may hire a nighttime caregiver so they can sleep without worry.

There is a clear licensing difference concerning what constitutes home companion care and what constitutes home health care, especially in North Carolina. But at the same time, Certified Nursing Assistants (CNA) or Personal Care Attendants (PCA) can provide hands-on *or* hands-off home care. It can sometimes be a little confusing. Some states, like Arizona and California, don't even require home care agencies to be licensed.

There are significant differences between home companion care and home health care, although people often use the terms interchangeably. To the medical profession, the home care profession, and even licensing and regulatory bodies, they mean entirely different things.

Companion caregivers themselves typically are not licensed; generally speaking, the qualifications are a willingness and ability to take care of the elderly and a clean background check. Often, companion caregivers don't have a personal care license or Certified Nursing Assistant (CNA) license, but are typically overseen by a Registered Nurse (RN) or social worker who provides a care plan of care to be followed. The nature of the care that they provide is completely non-medical.

Many people are surprised to learn that this type of care is typically not covered by health insurance. An exception might be if the client happens to have long-term care insurance. In that case, it may be covered in certain situations depending on the terms of the policy.

Read your long-term policy very carefully and speak with your insurance company representative to understand exactly what is covered.

### *Respite Care*

Respite care is typically used when somebody needs a rest from family caregiving duties. For example, Alex cares for her mother who has dementia. While Alex keeps her mother safe and cares for her mother's needs, life continues. She still has her own appointments to keep, shopping to do, and children to attend to. From time to time, it is important for her to just take a break, remove herself from her responsibilities, and nourish her soul. Anything from a walk in the park to a getaway vacation can help caregivers recharge their batteries and be better equipped for caregiving.

Professional caregivers can provide respite care for just a few hours or a whole week. These caregivers can visit clients in their homes, living facility, or hospital to provide emotional assistance, caregiver assisting, light housekeeping, and companionship. The level of service respite care provides can range from companion care all the way to hands-on care with a CNA or RN.

Respite care is typically not covered by health insurance either, but may be covered by long-term care insurance depending on the terms of the policy.

### *Personal Care Attendant (PCA) and Certified Nurse's Assistant (CNA) Care*

CNA's and PCA's typically help a client bathe, toilet, and shower, and can even brush a client's teeth. In addition, they can cut up food and feed clients their meals. Frequently, they are responsible for keeping a client's home clean and doing the shopping. They can even be responsible for doing laundry, mopping the floors, and keeping the bathroom clean (which can be a challenge if the client has toileting issues). Depending on the individual needs of the client, the duties of these caregivers can vary widely.

In many states, an RN must oversee a CNA, and a care plan must be in place for the client that specifies all aspects of hands on care and duties of the caregiver.

This type of care is usually not covered by health insurance even when persons are unable to go to the bathroom by themselves. Some state programs will cover it through Medicaid. It is a special state program though, and getting approval can be tricky. Someone may qualify for Medicaid but be on a waiting list for several years, which effectively means having to go to skilled nursing care.

CNA and PCA care is typically paid for out-of-pocket. If you have a long-term care policy, it may cover some costs.

### Hospice Care

Hospice organizations offer a variety of different care options for the dying and their loved ones. A hospice team of health care professionals, social workers, counselors, and volunteers work together to provide care, support, and comfort. They often have a doctor on staff and can provide CNA levels of care, such as bathing and dressing a client. They can also provide durable medical equipment like hospital beds and bedside commodes, much in the same way that home health care agencies can.

Generally speaking, hospice care is usually provided after a patient has been diagnosed with six months or less to live. The hospice agency may have volunteers who come in and sit with your loved one, but they generally don't provide an around-the-clock companion. Sometimes hospice care may not be enough care to cover all of a patient's needs. There may also be a need for additional home care to provide rest and respite for family caregivers.

## *Medication Reminders*

This service is simply a reminder to the client to take their medication: the person performing the medication reminder does not dispense the medication. They simply make sure that the medications in the current pillbox are being taken at the prescribed times. They can open and hand the client their medication box, but they cannot hand the patient the medication or put it in the patient's mouth. The caregiver giving reminders does not always know what the medicines are for—only what needs to be taken and when.

Companion caregivers who are not specifically licensed to provide medical care cannot administer injections. For clients with diabetes, non-medical caregivers can oversee clients drawing out their insulin but cannot draw it out or administer it to the client. This can create some issues if the client wants the caregiver to administer the injections for them or cannot get medications into their own mouth.

## *Transportation Services*

In most parts of the United States, we depend on being able to drive a vehicle to get around. Seniors often feel the need to continue driving to buy groceries, drive themselves to the doctor's office, or go to church on Sunday. When seniors feel they are no longer comfortable driving or when you see that they are no longer able to drive safely, it is time to find transportation alternatives for them.

Some communities offer bus service for a nominal charge during the week if a rider is able to work around the bus schedule, walk to, and stand at bus stops. A more convenient and safer option for seniors is to use a home care agency's transportation services. Some agencies provide transportation by transporting a client in the client's own vehicle. Occasionally, you will come across an agency like Extension of You that does provide vehicles for transporting clients, even clients using wheelchairs.

Extension of You has a wheelchair accessible vehicle which gives clients who must use a wheelchair the option to go out and do things that they might not otherwise be able to do. This transportation can open a world of opportunities for those using a wheelchair. They can easily be transported to doctor's appointments, the pharmacy, grocery shopping, or on any number of different types of trips they might need to make.

Transportation is usually not covered by insurance, but in some cases, Medicaid recipients can receive coverage.

The care a client can receive at home can be quite varied. It's important to be thorough in asking your provider questions, so you'll know exactly what kind of care and how much of it you are signing up for.

In summary:

- If a doctor recommends home health care, understand exactly what kind of help will be received.

- Don't assume that all needs are going to be covered.

- Don't make an assumption about how long a provider's services are going to be covered by insurance.

- Ask specifically how much time caregivers will spend with the client.

# Hiring a Home Care Provider

### *The Agency's Hiring Process*

For an agency's hiring process to be thorough, the following should be completed for each caregiver:

- 10-panel drug screen

- National criminal record and driving background check

- Registries checked for RNs and CNAs

- TB test

- References check

- In-depth, multi-stage interviews

The 10-panel drug screen provides greater assurance than a five-panel drug screen. It tests for abuse of both prescription and illegal drugs. Leaving a caregiver with drug issues alone with a senior who is taking all sorts of medications is bound to be a problem, and it's one of the reasons drug testing is so important. I've read about numerous cases of caregivers taking clients' medications. In addition to the drug screen at the beginning of hire, employers should require periodic, unannounced drug screens of their employees. Though an added expense for the agency, it's vitally important.

Because many home care clients—the elderly and the infirm—are vulnerable individuals, it is critical that agencies complete a background check when hiring an employee and continue with periodic rechecks. Amazingly, some caregivers being sent out by agencies have a criminal background record that the agency doesn't know about because they haven't done their due diligence.

My family had an experience that may have been avoided if the agency we hired had done periodic background checks. My mother had one particular caregiver taking care of her for several months. Eventually, we started noticing that things were missing. We did a simple Internet search and found that she had been arrested in the previous couple of months for shoplifting. Had the agency been diligent and performed background checks after their initial hiring process, they may have discovered this before we did. Because they didn't, they hired somebody with a police record. Do not just assume that an agency performs periodic background and drug screen checks; ask them about it.

By North Carolina state requirement, tuberculosis (TB) tests must be performed annually. This is also a requirement in most other states as well. Given that caregivers work in potentially high-risk situations, there is a potential that they may be exposed to TB. Annual checks help protect both the client and the caregiver.

### The Ball is in Your Court

You have to ask an agency: have you verified the caregiver's licensing status (if applicable) and completed a background check? Have you completed appropriate drug and medical testing? Ask the agency to see the training record of the caregiver they are providing to make sure that person really has the skillset you require.

To find an agency that meets your standards, ask a lot of questions about the agency's business model: How do they compensate their employees? How do they train them? Do they check applicants' references? How long do they retain information about caregivers? North Carolina and other states require this record keeping. Record keeping is important to you because you need to be able to go back and review those records if some sort of problem develops. You should know how long you would be able to come back for information if the need should arise (as in cases of litigation, unfortunately).

Ask how often the agency supervisor visits clients, and when they do so. Does the supervisor make sure to visit during every shift that is covered by caregivers, including second and third shifts?

### *Chemistry*

In-depth information gathering and interviewing of a potential employee should be part of the larger quality assurance plan by the employer. However, the interview process shouldn't be considered complete after someone is hired. From the client's point of view, this is the beginning of a relationship and should be approached with that mindset. An agency should ensure that caregivers are appropriately matched with clients to make sure they are compatible.

Some agencies simply send the first available caregiver out to a client. An agency that does it right will make sure that the client and the caregiver are a good fit. This is important because caregiving is very personal. Caregivers often help clients with intimate tasks in their home and in their lives. Client and caregiver are going to be together, often alone, for many hours on end. Getting a good fit includes ensuring that the two share a connection and are comfortable with each other. This cannot be stressed enough. Well-matched clients are happier and more satisfied: they thrive.

Good chemistry between the client and caregiver is an often-overlooked piece in this puzzle, but it shouldn't be. Clients should have the right to request or refuse specific caregivers. A good agency will ensure that there are always multiple caregivers, including back-up caregivers, who are acceptable to any given client.

An agency should spend a good amount of time getting to know a client's needs, personality, and how their family works together. An agency representative should make sure that the adjustment between the caregiver and the client is going well and that the family and client are satisfied with the caregiver's services.

There should be no single point of failure within an agency. You should know with whom to speak if you ever have a problem. There should be a clear chain of command. You should never experience being told something like, "Oops, sorry. Your RN is out of town for the weekend," or "We can't help you after 5:00 pm on Friday." The levels of responsibility and chain of command need to be very clear, as a client may have a problem at times outside of normal business hours.

## *Training*

Agencies should ensure that additional, ongoing training is provided to caregivers as needs, laws, and rules change. In this way, caregivers have the skills needed to properly care for their clients.

It can be very difficult for a caregiver to watch a client's health decline, especially a client with dementia. This makes it important for an agency to provide the adequate support, training, and coping strategies caregivers need to manage a client who is going through these changes. The information we have about Alzheimer's and dementia changes from year to year. It is important that caregivers are given updated training on a regular basis so that they can provide the best possible, up-to-date care for the client.

## *The Patient's Right to Choose*

In summary, you should only accept caregivers you like and who do a great job for you. You should choose the most appropriate level of care for your needs, and make sure that you receive what you require.

You shouldn't settle or accept second best for your loved one. No matter what level of care is required, your standards should always remain high.

For companion, personal, and other home care workers, your requirements can and should specify how they provide services to the client. That includes bathing and toileting preferences, how clothes are treated, and how often clothing and incontinence protection briefs are changed. You can and should specify how they take care of the home of your loved one while they are there. If you have a caregiver providing personal care services or companion care, the caregiver should take out the trash, vacuum, do general chores around the house, and make sure that things are well cared for.

Don't feel you are being overly demanding – it is your job to make sure that your parents' needs are completely met by an agency.

# Caregiver Supervision and Training

### *Oversight*

Every home care company will tell you that they supervise their employees very closely. They will say that they know exactly what is going on with their clients and that they are on top of every situation.

In my experience, reality is somewhat different. Many agencies only minimally supervise their caregivers and clients. For instance, Dad had a nighttime caregiver who by my own admission was fantastic. She took care of him overnight from 5:30 pm to 5:30 am for two years. During that time, she never once saw a supervisor during her work shift. That is two years with no supervisory visit! Fortunately for us, she was amazing. Still, there was absolutely no supervision or skill assessment of her work while she was taking care of my father. Can you imagine having a job that allows you to work for two years without ever having a supervisor evaluate your work?

The caregiver interacted with the office staff during the day, but there was never any contact while she was working with the client—my dad—to verify that the relationship was good and that everything was going as it should. A quality agency does not allow such a situation. Caregivers must be adequately supervised: ask a potential agency *how* they supervise their employees.

Good agency supervisors should make random, unannounced visits to the client's residence to assess the condition of the client and ensure that the appropriate level of care is being delivered. Sometimes problems can simmer quietly underneath the surface and can only be spotted with in-person visits. For example, maybe the caregiver is not taking out the trash, is not being attentive enough, or is having the client use a urinal and isn't cleaning up urine spills on the carpet.

There may be any number of reasons why the client doesn't complain, including that they don't notice there is a problem or that they may be afraid to say something. They could be afraid of abuse or of losing a cherished caregiver who is performing below standards. My own father failed to tell me when caregivers didn't change diapers or make sure he exercised. He didn't particularly care for the exercise anyway, so he didn't mind not having to exercise at all. Unfortunately, when he didn't stretch and exercise, he quickly lost the ability to even walk.

By North Carolina state law, agencies have to visit a client every three months to reevaluate and update his or her plan of care. However, that doesn't necessarily mean that they will visit each *caregiver* every three months; it just means that they are going to visit the *client* when any caregiver is present. That is an important distinction. If there is more than one caregiver for a patient, there is no guarantee that all caregivers will be assessed. This system allows caregivers to work for long stretches without having supervisory visits during their work shift. Imagine that you have an agency providing caregivers for two twelve-hour shifts per day. If the agency only goes out during the day, they will never observe the nighttime caregiver in action.

Ask an agency how often they evaluate each caregiver and what they assess: what is their entire process for each supervisory visit? It is important that these assessment visits are unannounced. You can learn a lot just by showing up when the caregiver is working. This may sound over-the-top, but I can tell you that I discovered a lot of things going on with my parents when I made surprise visits.

Extension of You Home Care lets our caregivers know that they will have unannounced evaluations at random times while they are working. They know we're appraising the quality of their work.

Because the agency we were using for my dad wasn't making unannounced supervisory visits, we did. During those visits, we discovered caregivers arriving late and leaving early; the time card system that their agency was using made that possible.

Random visits were also the way we found out that Dad had been allowed to drink alcohol. We wouldn't have noticed it had we not been there shortly after it happened. We realized what had happened because he would become confused and disoriented after consuming even just a half glass of wine.

I have seen caregivers who would come in and simply pour kitty litter on top of the kitty litter box rather than scoop it out. This created a mess and stunk up the entire apartment. We've had some who would not take out the trash as requested. That meant the entire apartment ended up smelling like soiled adult diapers. I discovered these kinds of things more often during visits when fill-in caregivers had been sent to Dad. He would have never told me had I not found out on my own. Honestly, I'm not sure he could have smelled the apartment or have remembered to tell me.

Appallingly, we found that he would sometimes be left unattended by his caregiver. We also discovered he was left to soil his incontinence protection brief and even encouraged to use it, rather than the caregiver helping him get up and use the toilet. Too often, that would result in a urinary tract infection.

Whenever he had a new caregiver, we learned that we had to make unannounced visits more frequently, because the agency wasn't providing training for each employee who worked with my father. I cannot overstate the importance of making sure that the agency makes unannounced visits and that the caregivers know that their supervisor is going to be randomly evaluating their performance. It is the best practice across all agencies, but something that most agencies simply don't have the staffing to handle. As a result, they don't actually follow through with proper supervision.

The truth of the matter is that pretty much everyone needs some degree of supervision in their job. A lack of supervision is unacceptable in a home care setting—the stakes are just too high. If you hire an agency, you are paying for an appropriate level of supervision of caregivers, and your standards should be met or exceeded.

### *Fear of Retribution*

In many instances, a client won't complain about a caregiver who is not doing a good job because they are afraid of retribution. They are afraid their caregiver will leave them and they will be left without any care, or they fear facing worse consequences at the hands of the caregiver. Those consequences can range from neglect to outright abuse, theft, or destruction of property. Retribution from caregivers can be a very real threat to clients, and an agency needs to make sure to supervise relationships closely to help prevent this from happening.

An agency needs to make sure that clients can come to them at any time with problems without having to fear mistreatment: a client needs to feel safe. The client and the client's children need to know that their problems are taken seriously and that they are addressed properly in every situation.

Because elderly clients are often vulnerable and fragile, it is of utmost importance that an agency is diligent about how it serves them.

Regular visits from an agency representative help establish a relationship between the client and agency. Having that relationship can help avoid problems entirely or at least allow them to be addressed early if they do arise.

### *Training*

There are different levels of skill among caregivers. Some assist with personal care appointments, and some assist with more involved care such as diapering, bathing, toileting, brushing teeth, dressing, feeding, ambulation, stretches, and blood pressure monitoring. A caregiver should always have the proper training required to care for a particular patient. For instance, some patients need a particular type of weight belt or physical therapy belt in order to be helped out of their chairs. If a caregiver has not received the proper training, she or he may try to grab the patient by their arms rather than the belt. That can lead to dislocated shoulders for the patient and an injured back for the caregiver.

You should also ensure that caregivers have received proper training in blood borne pathogens and universal precautions. If they haven't, they might be transferring illnesses or diseases back and forth between patients.

One simple policy that some agencies have is that their caregivers never go in and set their purses down directly on the client's counter. Bags and purses can carry germs from one patient to another. If a caregiver has a client who is sick, that caregiver has the potential to carry the illness to the next client. That means the caregiver can be a vector of illness transmission between clients, especially during cold and flu season.

Well-run agencies will have a supervisor who can train caregivers for specific situations and make sure they are following the necessary protocols—toileting protocols for example. We had a number of caregivers who allowed my dad to use a urinal at his chair, which meant that urine spilled all over his chair and all over the floor around the chair. Besides the mess, it was important that Dad got up and moved about; he needed to get up and *move* to use the toilet. He was happy to avoid getting up though whenever he could get away with it. With proper training, a caregiver should know better than to allow this to happen. It is vital to ensure that caregivers are trained and willing to perform the duties required to keep the patient clean and safe.

Agencies must oversee and train their caregivers carefully to ensure they are fully competent in all aspects of their job. Most agencies will retain proper records of training, but some do not. Some allow their caregivers' licenses to expire without being renewed. That happened at least three different times while CNAs worked for my family. That didn't mean that they didn't have the skills; what it meant was that the agency had not made sure that their licenses were properly renewed while they were working. That's just not good management and can be indicative of further problems.

### *Communication*

Something we use at Extension of You that provides both a level of supervision *and* communication is a written journal kept in the client's home or apartment. We use a simple notebook, similar to the bound composition books children use in school. Since the pages are permanently bound, there is no easy way to tear off a page without it being obvious that a page is missing. The journal allows family members and caregivers to communicate back and forth.

Caregivers can also communicate with each other as they work different shifts. When they begin their shift, they know to check the notes and see how the previous shift went. By reading the journal, caregivers should be able to easily confirm that the client has taken all of their medication. They can also check to see if a client has been having blood sugar spikes; the previous caregiver will have written down the numbers from blood sugar tests. Even if they are not measuring the client's blood sugar levels themselves, they can at least communicate their observations about their client's blood sugar levels.

With a journal, you record any problem a client is having including how long the problem has been happening so that the information can be easily forwarded to the client's doctor. This practice is a good way to detect health issues early. This simple journal ensures a continuity of care by the caregivers, and it has proven to be tremendously effective for both clients and their families.

*"Several wonderful Extension of You caregivers have become like a part of our family. They keep my father calm and entertained...and make copious notes for us, so we'll know what's going on when we're not able to be there."*
*- Tina, Cary, NC*

If your agency doesn't use a journal to track care, I highly recommend that you get this kind of notebook and make sure that the caregivers use it to write back and forth. At Extension of You, we have a binder that contains the journal, the client's current care plan, a pen, instructions, and any other information needed to care for the client. We keep emergency contact information in the binder as well. That way, we know exactly what the plan is and whom to call when urgent communications are necessary.

### *Supervising Your Independently Hired Caregiver*

If you want to hire a caregiver on your own, you too need to be making those random, unannounced visits to make sure that your loved one is being cared for properly. Please understand that if you hire your own independent caregiver, you must provide management of that caregiver in addition to on-site supervision to make sure that they are doing what they are supposed to do when they are supposed to do it. Nothing can substitute for in-depth supervision of employees.

***

When an agency provides adequate supervision and training to its employees, it relieves a tremendous amount of pressure from the family. Families of Extension of You clients say that the counseling and supervision we give our employees gives them peace of mind and eases their workload. Their need to make unexpected visits to ensure that the caregivers are doing their job is significantly less.

Why would you hire an agency if you have to do a large part of their job for them?

# Financial Considerations

Before she passed away, Mom never worked outside the home and had never been responsible for financial matters. Her ability to make spending decisions was poor, so we had to have a lot of discussions with her to help her understand her budget. We would have to say things like, "No, I'm sorry, Mom. You can't go shopping and spend a thousand dollars on clothes, because then Dad won't have enough money left to pay for your care."

Dad's ability to understand finances and how much money he did or didn't actually have also eroded over time. He could not understand the difference between 10 and 100, and he couldn't understand the concept of having to pay for his own care. He would periodically ask if he had enough money. He clearly didn't *like* spending money on his own care — he would have fits about it — but he was fine with spending large amounts of money on other things: expensive gifts for girlfriends he met after Mom passed away, expensive things for his grandchildren, or even a new car if he thought he wanted it. He had lost the ability to judge and make decisions based on his actual needs.

Legally, my parents had the authority to go out and make their own money decisions. However, if we hadn't taken control of the money, it would have all been gone long before my parents passed away. Telling them that they couldn't spend their own money was very difficult and disconcerting at times for me. My parents had always been the ones to create boundaries, set limits, and make their own decisions. Now the tables were turned, and while it wasn't easy for them, it wasn't easy for me either.

### Controlling Costs

As mentioned previously, most home care is not covered by health insurance. Medicare and many private health insurances won't pay for home care or nursing home care. Medicaid will pay for nursing home care if a client meets the guidelines set forth by the state.

The costs of around the clock care can be high. Many people cared for in skilled nursing facilities end up on Medicaid at the end of their lives, because they can no longer afford to pay for care. The facility that will accept Medicaid may not be the one you would have chosen given a greater variety of options. Therefore, anything that we can do as an agency that will help make a client's money go further is important. Sometimes we are able to offer creative care options to clients to help them afford staying at home longer. Sometimes with creative scheduling, different services can be combined: completing multiple errands in a single trip is much more affordable than separate trips.

Extension of You has many clients who use small blocks of time a few times a week. One client has us come in for three to four hours at a time. We take her to doctor appointments she has scheduled during these times, shopping, and any other errands she wants to do.

For those living in an independent living community, home care is generally much more affordable than having to move to a full-time care facility. Likewise, home care can be less expensive than moving to assisted living. Several hours a week of additional support can make the difference. As long as your loved ones don't need instant service at any given time and their needs can be scheduled, it may be feasible for them to remain in an independent living community or in your home with a caregiver who visits periodically.

### When Need for Care Increases

If your loved one has a condition such as Alzheimer's or advanced dementia, it is probably not feasible to have a caregiver who only visits occasionally. Persons with these types of conditions are at risk of wandering away or doing other things that put themselves in jeopardy. For example, they may turn on the stove and leave it on or fall and not able to call for help.

At first glance, it may seem that the cost of having a one-on-one, in-home caregiver around the clock is daunting. An important thing to remember is that your loved one is getting individual care that way. That's not really possible in a group setting. Most facilities have a one-to-six or one-to-eight ratio: six or eight patients for each staff member. If your loved one requires more individualized care than is provided by a facility, you should be able to bring in your own caregivers to help provide the extra level of attention you desire. Sometimes people need or want more attention than a facility can provide.

There may be times when you need to increase the level of home care for a short while. For example, you may want to have a caregiver in place around the clock to help with recovery from a surgery, illness, or a fall.

Or, perhaps you'll want to have a caregiver temporarily stay around the clock while you contemplate what level of services are needed and who will provide them. It's often difficult to know how long increased levels of care will be needed; that is why it's important to fully understand your and your parents' financial position when making care decisions.

### *Your Parents' Financial Position*

Keep in mind that in addition to monthly income, assets should be taken into consideration when determining finances available to pay for care. Any assets your parents own can be used to pay for their care. Talk to a certified financial planner to map out your parents' finances and understand what their available cash flow could be.

If you are moving your parent to a care community, funds from the sale of their house can be used to pay for the care. If you are contemplating big moves like this with your parents' finances, it is critical that you understand exactly what everyone's rights and responsibilities are.

If you are making decisions for your parents, you'll need to have proper legal authority: power of attorney, health care power of attorney, and a living will. Sometimes there are conflicts between children of parents in need of care. In these situations it is important to be open to negotiating, keeping in mind what your parents would have wanted and what is actually feasible. Sometimes it helps to have an attorney involved to make sure that legal matters are taken care of properly.

I encourage you to look at the subject of finances very carefully. It is important to understand you parents' finances early on and to re-evaluate them from time to time. Understand that everything might not be as it appears —sometimes, aging parents will over or understate their financial situation. Being cautious and organized will help you have a better understanding of which care options are available to you.

Some clients don't like being faced with the fact that they have to pay for their own care. This was a huge deal with my father. He did not understand that he had funds to pay for care for years and frankly, he just didn't *want* to pay for it. He preferred to receive all of his care from me. Unfortunately, it was at a time when I had an infant to care for and a full-time job outside the home as well. My providing full-time care for Dad just wasn't an option. I also recognized that I was not the best caregiver for the situation, especially considering that he had dementia and other complications.

Have your family sit down together and think about what your parents' needs are: be compassionate about them, and understand that your parents are probably not going to be happy about having to spend money on care. Most likely, they have been conditioned to be thrifty. That's a generational thing that has to be taken into account. In this situation, it is helpful to take a peaceful and creative approach. Ask for everyone's input and try to think of different alternatives before making a final decision.

Over the years, Dad and I had many clashes as he resisted care. Most of his resistance was to the cost of care. He was very much conditioned to not want to pay for any sort of care, medical needs, or the like. To him, the idea of having to pay thousands of dollars per month for someone to take care of my mother around the clock was ludicrous. My parents would have caregivers for a few months, and then Dad would decide he was spending too much money and let the caregiver go. At that point, both of my parents' health would decline as they ate more highly processed foods and generally were unable to take care of themselves. Eventually, their situation would evolve into a crisis that usually resulted in one of them ending up on a hospital. Then the cycle would repeat itself. I was finally able to break the cycle after my dad experienced a fracture in his back and ended up in a skilled nursing facility. Seeing that my mother was by herself at home, I quickly got her moved into a senior community and arranged for her caregiver to continue visiting her there. That way, I was able to ensure that they both had care. Because I wasn't being constantly called to take care of issues, I was also able to make sure I kept my job.

As dementia progresses, adult children often make substantial sacrifices to care for their parents. We love our parents and want to do our best for them, but the responsibilities can sometimes become overwhelming. By moving my mom and later my dad to an independent living community, I was able to help them maintain their finances, their standard of living, and my sanity.

# Employee Classification and Compensation and Why You Should Care

### *Employee or Independent Contractor?*

Most home care agencies treat their employees as independent contractors to reduce costs and avoid a variety of legal obligations. When they classify workers as independent contractors, they avoid providing benefits and paying social security, Medicare, and federal unemployment insurance on those employees. This can create problems down the line.

Federal statutes don't really provide a clear-cut definition of what constitutes an employee versus an independent contractor, but the more an employer controls when and where someone works and tells them what to do and how to do it, the more likely that worker is to be classified as an employee instead of an independent contractor. Interestingly, agencies do exercise that kind of control with their caregivers. According to this definition, an agency should be withholding taxes and social security for their employees. What this often boils down to is that many caregivers do not file or pay their taxes. When they are made aware that they owe a large amount of taxes, they may abruptly quit their position and leave your loved one without a caregiver. From a societal perspective, their contributions to Social Security are significantly lower, resulting in lower income and higher poverty during the caregiver's retirement.

If you are considering using a home care agency, it's likely that part of your motivation is to avoid employee/employer responsibilities. Therefore, one of the things you need to ask any agency is whether they are properly withholding for their employees.

Another thing to note is that most home care agencies do not offer their caregivers any paid time off or sick leave. It stands to reason that an agency that offers these benefits is going to attract more highly qualified talent—and isn't that what you really want? Unfortunately, paid time off is essentially unheard of in this industry.

So why would this matter to you? Our agency tells employees not to come to work when they are sick. I am sure every agency out there does the same, but how are they going to compel employees not to come to work sick when the employees' bills don't get paid if they don't work? As a result, employees come to work sick.

Most clients are elderly, and most are more susceptible to illnesses. They are what the medical community calls immune system compromised. That means they are much more likely to catch a cold or the flu. Unfortunately, what may be a minor sickness for an otherwise healthy adult can be life threatening for someone who is in a weakened or compromised state of health. To be blunt, having employees working while sick can result in significant illness for a client: illness that can require hospitalization or even result in death.

Steps should be taken to ensure that an employee who is running a fever, has a serious cough, is vomiting, or has diarrhea doesn't come to work. Caregivers should be nowhere near clients when they are in that state. It stands to reason that caregivers who have paid sick time are less likely to work while sick.

## Compensation

Many home care agencies pay their employees as little as possible. They may charge clients between 20 and 35 dollars an hour, depending on the client's age, geographic location, and other factors, while only paying the employee minimum wage. As a result, employees have to work much longer hours in order to make ends meet. Some have two jobs or work as many hours straight as they can. One of my dad's caregivers worked 12-hour days, seven days a week. That's 84 hours a week. How much time do you think she had to take care of herself or spend time with her family?

One of the things that we discovered with Mom and Dad's caregivers was that they constantly complained about their salary. They were very well aware of how much the agency was charging per hour, and many of them made certain that my parents knew that they were not receiving health insurance or adequate compensation. We heard comments like, "Well, you are paying this much, but we are making less than half of that." Moreover, turnover at many agencies approaches seventy percent per year. That means your loved one may experience a revolving door of caregivers. Even when over-worked and under-paid caregivers are providing adequate care to the client, there is usually an underlying attitude of dissatisfaction.

It will be helpful to your parent if you address employee pay and benefits up front. It's better to start out in a relationship knowing that an employee is being compensated fairly. It benefits your parent because they won't have to be uncomfortable listening to a disgruntled employee who saw their agency's billing and know that they got paid such a small percentage of it.

Not surprisingly, many caregivers are actively looking for another job. They may love their clients—and some of them would do nearly anything for their clients—but many caregivers are looking for something that will pay more per hour. Even if the raise is fifty cents per hour, they may jump on the opportunity because it can offer a significant improvement in their quality of life.

When employees are paid a decent wage, offered a 401K, given some paid time off, are paid for overtime, and are educated about finances and financial management, they can establish a foundation for long-term improvement in their life. It is paramount that clients be well cared for, but employees also need to be cared for so they can do a good job taking care of their clients.

Another form of compensation not usually talked about is education. I believe strongly in education. I myself went back for a Masters in Business Administration (MBA) and completed Certified Senior Advisor certification in my late thirties and early forties.

At Extension of You, we require all our employees to keep their certification current. By making sure that certificates do not lapse, we help ensure that our employees are able to find a comparable position at a different agency if the need arises. Certification is an important part of providing exemplary care, but requiring that it be maintained also shows employees that we value their skills and abilities and that they can be proud of being part of a high quality organization. The agency one of my dad's caregivers worked for allowed her CNA certifications to expire. If certifications are expiring, one has to wonder if a caregiver is receiving the necessary ongoing training. That particular CNA had a rough time regaining her certification after my dad passed away and almost had to start the certification process over again from the beginning.

We also encourage employees to take continuing education classes (CEU's) that our certified trainers teach, or we send them to appropriate classes. This helps them keep their licenses up to date and be able to provide the very best care. Providing continuing education also helps employees feel valued and keeps them engaged.

Extension of You employees naturally have the freedom to leave the agency at any time, but I believe that if we offer them adequate wages and treat them well, they will choose not to leave. That means less turnover and better-trained employees. Employees who feel valued will most likely be more loyal to their clients and employer, which directly correlates to improved outcomes for clients.

### *Billing*

Some agencies bill chunks of hours instead of the actual hours worked by a caregiver. Instead of billing you for the seven hours and 41 minutes that the caregiver was actually on site, they might bill for eight hours. Ask an agency what their policy is.

Many agencies in the market still use paper time cards instead of GPS or telephony (which requires the caregiver to clock in using their client's home phone). Because telephony software can identify the number from which the call is made, it is simple to verify that the caregiver is indeed at the client's location. It's extremely easy for caregivers to forge paper time cards. They are able to claim hours worked at their own discretion. Clients may sign it even if it is incorrect, because they are afraid, have trouble reading the timecard, or don't really understand what they are signing. Make sure you understand and agree with how an agency will be billing for services.

### Hiring Your Own Caregiver Independently

If you hire a caregiver through an agency, you may find yourself wanting to hire them away from the agency to work for you independently. That is always a possibility, but you have to buy out the caregiver. When you do that, you essentially end up paying the agency a finder's fee for the employee and for dismissing the agency. If you do buy out a caregiver from an agency, you end up assuming the management role. You must provide supervision and manage payroll for your employee.

Some clients hire caregivers on their own (without using an agency) to save money. However, when you hire an agency, you reduce your responsibilities. Agencies handle the interviewing process, pay employer taxes, and report taxes. The agency also handles liability insurance, Workers Compensation, professional insurance, and bonding of the employee. If you hire someone on your own, you are responsible for these components.

Be aware that federal law requires you to withhold taxes if you have a domestic employee working in your house and earning more than a certain amount each month. There are significant accounting requirements for withholding and paying quarterly payroll taxes. Many individuals who independently hire caregivers and do observe legal regulations end up needing to hire an accountant.

Employees who have taxes withheld properly are contributing to Social Security. That's better for them in the long term because they are entitled to collect greater Social Security benefits when they retire.

***

Caring for employees responsibly has a cascade effect that makes it worth doing. It's like an ecosystem; anything you do in one part of the ecosystem affects the other parts. Actions and decisions are not made in a vacuum — they impact the health of a whole organization.

# Finding the Right Agency

The home care business can be very lucrative. According to AARP's website, about 8,000 people a day are turning 65 as the baby boomer generation ages. As a result, there are a ton of opportunists in the market as well as a ton of opportunities for them to get into the business of caring for seniors.

In fact, North Carolina had such rampant abuse in its home care system that a three-year moratorium on home care licenses was issued in 2011. In fact, the moratorium was just extended another two years, to expire in 2016. The state sees the need to make sure that agencies are properly licensed, have proper oversight, and are doing a decent job taking care of their clients. It has been tremendously difficult for the Department of Health and Human Services in North Carolina to catch up with the backlog of issues in the home care industry. Some states are getting around the backlog of licensing issues by requiring agencies in their states to obtain accreditation through an outside organization. As of now, that has not happened in North Carolina.

When you are searching for a quality agency, I encourage you to ask friends for referrals and listen to what they are saying. Speak with current agency clients and the caregivers themselves to get first-hand information.

Find out what you can about an agency's reputation. Look online, find their company website and Facebook page, and examine what they post. You can tell a lot about an agency from their tone and the information available on their website. Some will give you a lot more information about the industry than others—they want to help you be an informed customer. That can tell you something about how the company operates. Some states also have a license registry you can search to see if there are any violations for a particular agency.

When you call to interview an agency and talk to the nurse on duty and the manager of that particular agency, how are they responding your needs? Are they responding quickly? Are they following up with you? Do they do what they say they are going to do? Think hard about an agency that doesn't. Agencies should follow through with exactly what they say they are going to do. Don't settle for less. You have to be your family's best advocate for care.

With Dad, we discovered that having the right caregiver was crucial for his continued health. I could tell dozens of stories about caregiving gone wrong—from the caregiver who wanted to marry my dad shortly after my mom's death to the one who allowed him to have alcohol. Dad was an alcoholic *and* the alcohol reacted very badly with all of the medications he was on for Parkinson's. We have plenty of emotional scars to show for the experience.

Sometimes when we had a fill-in caregiver, there were days that Dad would not get up and do his physical therapy. He would not bother to walk the halls because he was not being made to do so. We would immediately see the negative effects on his mental capacity as well: there is a strong correlation between exercise and mental capacities.

We discovered that with the right caregiver, Dad got up, he exercised, he did physical therapy, and his overall physical and mental condition improved dramatically. With the right caregivers in place, we were even able to take a couple of family vacations. Those priceless opportunities might never have happened otherwise.

What this means for you and your loved one is this: if your agency can hire and retain the best caregivers, you will get the best possible care and have the best stability and outcome.

### *Ask the Right Questions*

Through trial and error, I have learned which questions to ask. Building a checklist is a good way to ensure that you ask the right questions. It will help you define the criteria that define good care for you.

Here are some questions you might want to begin with. Tailor this list to your and your parents' individual needs.

1. What is your hiring process?

2. Do you complete background checks that include driving and credit histories? Do you verify references and have proof of current TB testing?

3. Do you continue to do periodic background checks on employees? How often?

4. Can you show verification of licensing, multistate background, and drug test checks?

5. Do you randomly drug test employees? What type of test do you perform? How often are they tested?

6. How do you supervise your employees?

7. How do you track and bill caregiver hours?

8. How do you compensate your employees?

9. How do you train employees, and do you ensure that employees' licensing remains valid?

10. What insurance does your agency carry? (Expect worker's compensation, liability insurance, and bonding or third-party theft insurance)

11. What do you do if a caregiver is out sick or does not show up for their appointed shift?

12. Do you require a contract?

# Learn To Be An Advocate

As you have read, I have plenty of stories to tell about times my dad was not cared for properly. I do understand that even with the best intentions and precautions, sometimes things go wrong. But knowledge is power. Learning what is expected and required of a quality caregiver can mean the difference between getting great care and being mistreated or taken advantage of. Over time, I learned that it was crucial for me to become an informed advocate concerning Dad's care. I became a better consumer for myself and for my father—I only wish I had known how to do it earlier in the process.

Remember to be mindful of personal chemistry—or how you *feel*—when choosing a caregiver. Because caregivers are providing such intimate services, I believe clients should have the ultimate choice about which caregiver is coming into their home. If an agency doesn't give you a choice of caregivers, you might want to consider interviewing another agency. Even though you may be the one making the decisions, remember that your parents should also be comfortable with their caregivers. Otherwise, you may have a parent refusing to use the bathroom when they should and having accidents. My dad actually did this with one of his caregivers because he was romantically interested in her, and he was embarrassed to have her help him go to the toilet.

I encourage you to learn from my mistakes: I made plenty of them through years of taking care of both my parents. I've shared some of them in this book, but there are plenty more. I learned from them and so can you.

Remember who the customer is. Consumers have rights. They have the right to receive quality care at a fair price, they have the right to decide who takes care of their loved ones, and they have the right to expect a reasonable standard of care.

Understand that everybody's needs are not going to be the same, and you should be very specific about what your parent wants. With a healthcare provider's approval, if your mom likes collard greens, she should have collard greens. If your dad likes barbeque, then he should get barbeque. Dad loved spicy Mexican food — the more jalapeños on it, the better. We made sure that he got it on a regular basis. We also made sure that he was dressed in the clothing that he was the most comfortable and happiest in. It was important to my family that my dad was kept clean, dry, neat, and presentable at all times, rather than being left in dirty or unkempt clothes.

Make your specific wishes known to the agency. Make them the focus of how the agency provides service. Be a customer who is informed and, to some extent, demanding. Politely but firmly make sure that your parents' rights and needs are taken care of.

If you think that a caregiver is not performing up to your standards, call the agency. Ask that the caregiver be removed from the case immediately. Most agencies can and will provide another caregiver fairly quickly.

Don't be afraid to intervene, and don't be afraid to ask a lot of questions. Ask questions about what your mom ate for lunch and how she ate her lunch. Is she able to feed herself? Has the caregiver noticed any changes? What do they think about how she is doing?

Understand that caregivers are humans and the agencies that employ them are too, so they are fallible—we all are. If you say something once, you might have to say it again to make sure you've been understood. Being your parents' advocate and standing up for what you expect is vital to receiving the best possible care.

Becoming educated about all these issues can be challenging—especially if you haven't thought much about being in this position in the first place. This may be totally new for you. Like a lot of things in life, if you take the time to ask questions and become an educated consumer, you'll more likely be satisfied with what you get.

Best wishes on the voyage ahead. May you and yours be happy, healthy, safe, and filled with loving kindness.